Technology in the Time of
The Aztecs

Nina Morgan

RSVP

**RAINTREE
STECK-VAUGHN**
P U B L I S H E R S
The Steck-Vaughn Company

Austin, Texas

Titles in the Series

Ancient Egypt   **The Aztecs**

Ancient Greece   **The Maya**

Ancient Rome   **The Vikings**

Cover picture: An Aztec weaver works at her backstrap loom.
Title page: Aztec craftspeople at work, from a mural by Diego Rivera

Published by Raintree Steck-Vaughn Publishers,
an imprint of Steck-Vaughn Company

Library of Congress Cataloging-in-Publication Data
Morgan, Nina.
Technology in the time of the Aztecs / Nina Morgan.
    p.   cm.
    Includes bibliographical references and index.
    Summary: Examines the many aspects of culture
    in the Aztec society, including their food, clothes,
    buildings, industry, transport, warfare, and technology.
    ISBN 0-8172-4878-1
    1. Aztecs—Material culture—Juvenile literature.
    2. Aztecs—History—Juvenile literature.
    3. Aztecs—Social life and customs—Juvenile literature.
    [1. Aztecs. 2. Indians of Mexico.]
    I. Title.
    F1219.76.M37M67   1997
    972'.018—dc21   97-19066

Printed in Italy. Bound in the United States.
1 2 3 4 5 6 7 8 9 0 02 01 00 99 98

Contents

Introduction

When the Spanish explorer Hernando Cortés led an army to Mexico in 1519 and met the Aztecs, he was amazed by what he found. "When we saw all those cities and villages built in the water, and other great towns on dry land ... we were astounded," wrote one of his soldiers. "Indeed, some of our soldiers asked whether it was not all a dream."

The center of the Aztec empire was in the Valley of Mexico. This is a high area with several large lakes, surrounded by mountains. When Cortés arrived, about one million Aztecs were living in villages, towns, and cities built around one of these lakes, Lake Texcoco.

Some of the towns were built on dry land, but others, like the Aztec capital Tenochtitlán (now Mexico City), were built on islands or on swampy marshland. Tenochtitlán was an impressive city. It was far bigger than any European city of the time, and it was very well organized.

The temple complex in the city of Teotihuacán, in the Valley of Mexico near Tenochtitlán.

4

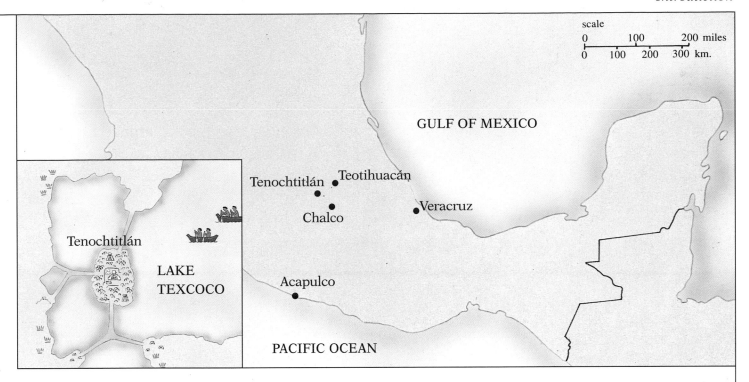

GULF OF MEXICO

Tenochtitlán • Teotihuacán

• Chalco

•Veracruz

Acapulco
•

PACIFIC OCEAN

Tenochtitlán

LAKE TEXCOCO

Tenochtitlán was linked to the mainland by three raised roads, or causeways. There were few streets in the city. Instead, the Aztecs built a regular grid of canals so that people could travel around the city and transport goods by boat.

The Aztecs grew food in gardens, which were laid out in the marshes on the outskirts of the city. They organized a system to supply clean water for drinking. Merchants traveled far and wide in central America to bring back goods and raw materials, which were bought and sold in busy markets.

In the center of Tenochtitlán and other large cities were splendid temples and beautifully decorated public buildings. Important Aztecs, such as priests and nobles, lived in houses built around courtyards close to the center, while ordinary people lived in smaller houses built along canals on the outskirts of the city.

Technology in Aztec times depended more on human skills than on tools and machines. Although they had no iron tools or carts with wheels, and no alphabet, the Aztecs managed to build a highly developed civilization in just two hundred years. The secret of their success was that they learned to use very simple tools with great skill. The Aztec legacy lives on in Mexico.

A map of Mexico at the time of the Aztecs. Inset: the city of Tenochtitlán, built on Lake Texcoco.

Food

Producing Food

Aztec farmers had no plows or carts and no working animals to pull them. Instead, they relied on simple tools and hard work to grow their food.

The Aztecs ate very well. Their most important food was corn. Tomatoes, avocados, chilies, peppers, sweet potatoes, pineapples, chocolate, pumpkins, and peanuts were also important in their diet. These fruits and vegetables were all new to the invading Spaniards, but they soon learned to like them. Spanish ships carried many of these foods back to Spain, and they soon became part of the European diet.

"Floating" Farms

In the marshland around Tenochtitlán the Aztecs grew their food in "floating" gardens called *chinampas*. These gardens did not really float; they were narrow strips of land, separated by canals.

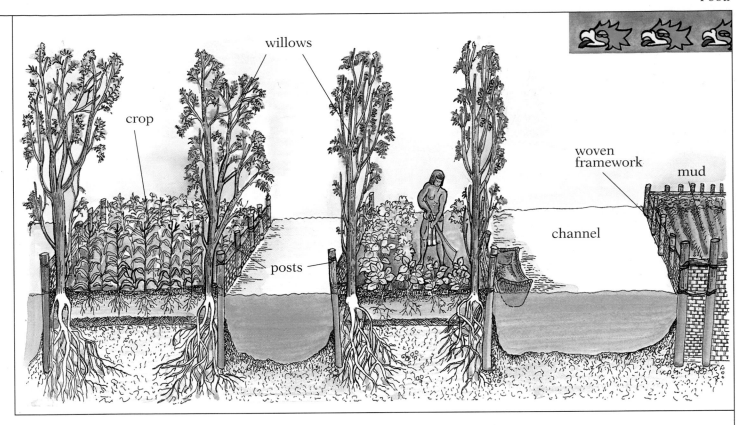

willows

crop

posts

woven framework

mud

channel

Building *Chinampas*

Farmers built their *chinampas* by digging channels through the marshes and heaping up mud to create small islands. To keep the mud from washing away, they sank wooden posts at each end of the island and built a framework of woven sticks around the sides. They also planted willow trees at each corner so that the tree roots would help to keep the soil in place. To keep the soil on the *chinampas* fertile, the farmers spread fresh mud from the lake over their gardens. They also dug in plenty of animal and human manure—human waste was collected from special boats moored at various places that were used as public lavatories. Thanks to this treatment, the soil on the *chinampas* was so rich that farmers could grow up to seven crops each year.

Irrigating Fields

Not all farms were in the fertile swamps where it was easy to water plants. Farmers away from the marshes dug ditches to bring water from nearby streams to their fields.

Growing Crops

The most important food crop was corn, and the most useful farming tool was a digging stick called a *coa*. This was a broad wooden blade with a long handle. Farmers used *coas* for digging and hoeing, but it was hard work, which is why most Aztec farms were on light soil that was easy to dig.

Preparing Food

The Aztecs ate mostly fresh food, which they bought in the markets every day. They also preserved food to keep it from spoiling. The Aztecs did not use ovens but cooked their food on open fires. Ordinary people usually drank water, but for important Aztecs there were other drinks. A favorite was *choclatl*, or drinking chocolate, made from the beans of the cacao tree. *Octli*, an alcoholic drink made from the sap of the maguey cactus, was drunk by older Aztecs—only people over the age of thirty were allowed to drink alcohol.

Turning Corn into Flour

Turning the corn into flour was women's work and took many hours. The kernels had to be scraped off the cobs and soaked overnight in water mixed with limestone, to loosen the outer skins. In the morning the kernels were boiled and the skins removed. They were now soft enough to be ground into flour by crushing between a grooved stone roller (a *manos*) and a small stone slab (a *metate*).

Cooking

The Aztecs cooked on fires, which were lit in hearths inside their houses. Three stones were arranged in a triangle in the hearth and supported the cooking pots and pans. The stones also supported a flat stone griddle.

18.

Preserving Food and Storing It

The Aztecs preserved food by salting it or drying it in the sun. They stored the dried and salted food in pottery jars or special bins made of strips of wood or woven twigs plastered with mud. To salt food, they collected salty earth from around the lakes during the dry season and soaked it in water to dissolve the salt. The salty water, or brine, was then heated in pottery jars until the water boiled away, leaving salt crystals, which could be kept in jars or pressed into blocks.

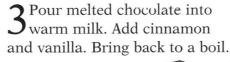

Make an Aztec Drink

You need a double boiler, a saucepan, a wooden spoon, a measuring cup, and a whisk. Ingredients: 8 oz. (225 g) of dark cooking chocolate, 1 qt. (1 l) of milk, 1/4 teaspoon of ground cinnamon, and 2 drops of vanilla. Ask an adult to help you with the stove and hot pans.

1 Break chocolate into small pieces and put it in top of double boiler. Fill bottom with cold water, bring it to a boil, then turn heat down so it boils gently. Stir chocolate with wooden spoon until melted.

2 Pour milk into other saucepan and heat gently—don't let it boil.

3 Pour melted chocolate into warm milk. Add cinnamon and vanilla. Bring back to a boil.

4 Turn heat down and whisk the mixture for two minutes until it foams. Pour into four mugs and serve.

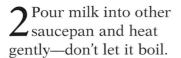

Clothes

Spinning and Dyeing

Aztec women developed and used the technology to spin fibers, weave and dye cloth, and design and sew clothing. Aztec clothes were very simple. Men wore loincloths, sometimes with cloaks. Women wore long skirts and simple blouses. Clothes worn for special occasions were decorated with embroidery.

Yarns from Cactus Leaves

The Aztecs used the strong, coarse fibers of the maguey cactus to weave cloth for everyday clothes. To prepare the fibers, they first heated the cactus leaves over a fire. Then, they soaked them in water and beat them to loosen the fibers. They scraped the fibers off the leaves, washed them, and squeezed them dry. For better-quality cloth, the Aztecs used cotton. First, they separated the cotton fibers from the seeds and combed out the short and useless fibers. For luxury clothing, they spun rabbit fur or even feathers into yarns and wove them together with cotton thread.

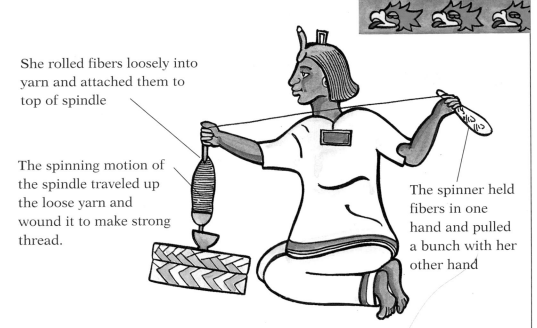

Spinning

Aztec women used a spindle to spin yarn from fibers. This tool was made from a stick about a foot (30 cm) long. The lower end was put through a hole in the center of a clay disk, or spindle whorl. The spindle whorl worked like a toy top to help the spindle spin faster and for a longer time. Sometimes the bottom of the spindle was held in a small pottery cup. This helped it spin more freely.

She rolled fibers loosely into yarn and attached them to top of spindle

The spinning motion of the spindle traveled up the loose yarn and wound it to make strong thread.

The spinner held fibers in one hand and pulled a bunch with her other hand

Making Dyes

The Aztecs dyed their yarns before weaving them. To make their dyes, they soaked various plants, seeds, and insects in water; green came from the leaves of matlalquauitl and blue from indigo. They used the seeds of the anatta plant (shown here) for a rusty red color, and cultivated cochineal insects on prickly pear leaves, crushing their bodies to produce bright red dye.

Dyeing the Yarns

This painting by the Mexican artist Diego Rivera shows what an Aztec workshop may have looked like. The Aztecs dipped the yarns in vats of dye and stirred. Then they soaked them in alum or urine to fix the dye and stop the color from washing out. Many of the dyes used by the Aztecs are still used by weavers in Mexico today.

Weaving, Sewing, and Shoemaking

Aztec women used simple backstrap looms, still used for weaving in many parts of the world. On this type of loom the warp threads, or threads that run through the length of the cloth, are stretched between two poles called the warp beams. One of the warp beams is tied to a tree. The other beam has a belt or cloth strip attached to it for the weaver to put around her waist. The weaver sat away from the tree and leaned back to pull the warp threads tight.

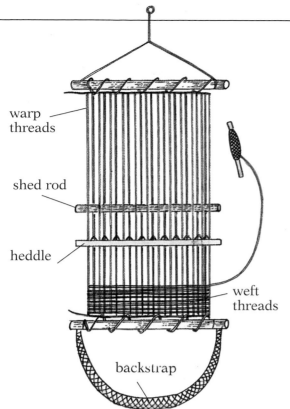

warp threads

shed rod

heddle

weft threads

backstrap

Weaving and Sewing

The weaver passed the weft in and out of the warp. To speed up weaving, Aztec weavers used a shed rod and a heddle. The shed rod was a round stick woven in and out of the warp threads. This made a passage, called a shed, for the weft thread to pass through. The heddle was used to raise and lower the warp threads. It was made out of a stick with long loops of thread, called leashes, attached to it. The heddle was placed on top of the warp, and leashes were tied around every other warp thread so that when the heddle was lifted, different groups of warp threads were raised. Once the cloth was woven, several widths had to be sewn together to make a piece of material wide enough for clothes. The spines of the maguey cactus were used for needles.

Aztec Sandals

Only important people and warriors wore sandals. The soles of this noble's sandals were made of treated animal skins or of the strong fibers of the maguey cactus twisted together. The cords that held his sandals around the big and first toes were also made of maguey fibers. Sometimes the cords went around the heel or were wound up the leg from ankle to knee.

Make an Aztec Skirt

You can make this simple Aztec skirt by sewing just one seam. To make it you need a piece of cloth about 3 ft. (1 m) square (a bath towel or tablecloth is ideal), a long strip of cloth to use as a belt, and a needle and thread.

1 Fold the cloth in half and sew the side edges together to make a tube. Turn the tube inside out so the seam doesn't show.

2 Step into the tube and pull it up so that the bottom edge reaches your ankles.

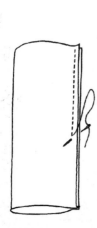

3 Use the cloth strip as a belt and tie it around your waist to hold the skirt up. Fold the top of the skirt over the belt to make a neat waistband. You can embroider the bottom of the skirt with a design.

Buildings

Homes, Pyramids, and Temples

The Aztecs had good reason to be proud of their capital city. When Cortés and his soldiers arrived, they were amazed to find that Tenochtitlán was far bigger than any European city. More than 250,000 people lived there. There were palaces, law courts, public baths, and markets. Many houses were built on raised platforms to protect them from floods. Most were just one story high, because taller houses would have been too heavy to stand on the marshy ground.

Causeways, Bridges, and Aqueducts

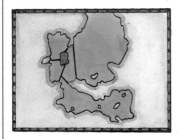

The Aztecs built three wide causeways to connect Tenochtitlán to the mainland. These were of stone, supported on wooden pillars. They built the causeways with gaps joined by wooden bridges that could be removed to allow canoes to pass through and to keep enemies out. Other wooden bridges over canals in the city were permanent. Two stone aqueducts brought fresh water into Tenochtitlán from springs in the surrounding hills. These had two clay pipes so that when one was being cleaned or repaired the other could carry water. In some places the aqueducts opened out to form reservoirs.

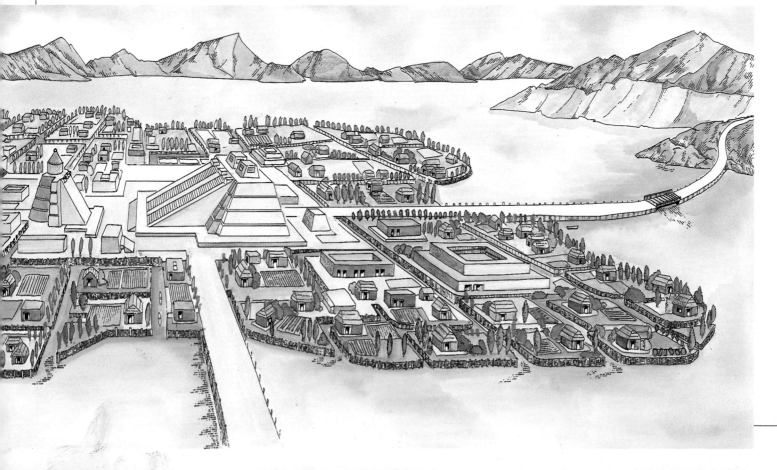

Pyramids and Temples

Temples were among the most important buildings in Aztec towns. They were built on top of pyramids, usually on a platform made by leveling off the top of the pyramid. The pyramid rose in terraces with a broad stairway leading to the temple at the top. Important temples had roofs made of wooden beams forming a point. These were covered with sticks and twigs and coated with a plaster made of mud and animal dung to keep out the rain.

Transporting Building Materials

The Aztecs had to carry all the stone and large pieces of wood they used in their buildings. Builders carried smaller materials in large cone-shaped baskets, called *chundi*, on their backs and supported the heavy load using a strap across their foreheads. We do not know how the Aztecs moved blocks of stone or wood that were too heavy to carry. They did not have carts with wheels, so they must have found ways to use sleds, levers, and ropes, or rollers made from tree trunks to haul large blocks.

Building Tools

Aztec tools for crushing and hammering had wooden shafts and stone heads. Their axes and other cutting tools had copper blades. Chisels, hammers, and scrapers were often made of volcanic rock because this type of stone was very hard and strong. They often used obsidian, a glassy volcanic stone, because it could be shaped to a very sharp edge, and pumice, another type of volcanic rock, for drilling, grinding, and polishing.

Building on a Marsh

To prevent heavy buildings from sinking into the soggy soil of Tenochtitlán, the Aztec builders needed ways of supporting their constructions. To do this, they used foundation piles. Later the Spaniards used the same technology. Archaeologists can recognize the Spanish piles because the pointed ends were cut with metal tools.

Building the City

Because the land was marshy, buildings of Tenochitlán had to have firm foundations. One way the Aztecs used to do this was to drive large wooden stakes, 3 to 4 in. (8 to 10 cm) in diameter, and more than 30 ft. (9 m) long, into the soggy ground. The stakes were sharpened to a point at one end to make them easier to drive in. The builders pushed the stakes close together in the marsh to form a foundation for the walls of buildings. Another way the Aztecs solved the problem of building on soggy soil was to build new buildings over the ruins of older ones. The broken pieces from the older buildings helped stabilize the marshy ground in the same way that putting broken rocks or gravel on a muddy patch of road helps make it firmer. Once a firm foundation had been laid, Aztec builders and masons set to work building their splendid city.

Houses for Rich and Poor

Important Aztecs lived in houses with walls made of stone or adobe—a type of sun-dried clay. Their houses had many rooms built around a central courtyard. Doors were simply openings in the walls, and there were no windows. The roofs were flat and made of wooden beams covered with planks or smaller pieces of wood. On the outskirts of Tenochtitlán and in the countryside, ordinary people lived in huts with wattle walls and roofs thatched with maguey cactus leaves.

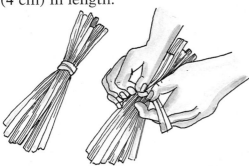

Make a Thatched "Roof"

Thatching is a simple technology that uses cheap materials and works well to keep out wind, rain, and sun.

You need a small piece of plastic or wooden grid. Plastic tile spacers are often sold stuck together in grids and are ideal for this project. You also need a handful of dry straw, wire twist-ties (used with plastic food storage bags), and scissors.

1 Sort the straw and lay the blades out side by side. Gather together 12 small bunches of straw and bind them at the top by wrapping a twist-tie around them, leaving the ends of the twist free. Trim the untied ends of the bunches of straw to about 1.5 in. (4 cm) in length.

2 On the bottom of the grid, tie on three bunches—one per square.

3 For the second row, go up two squares and tie three more bunches so that they fill in the gaps in the first row. Do the same for the third and fourth rows, so that an area of the grid is covered with the thatch bundles.

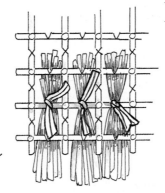

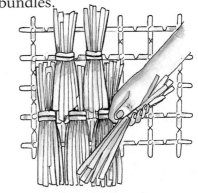

Try holding your thatch panel at an angle under a slowly running faucet to see what happens to the water.

17

Industry

Mining and Minerals

When the German artist Albrecht Dürer visited an exhibition in 1520 to see some of the treasures brought back by the Spaniards from the court of the Aztec emperor, Montezuma, he was very impressed. "I saw amazing objects and I marveled at the [skill] of the men in these distant lands," he wrote in his notebook. But although the Aztecs could make beautiful metal objects, the technology they used was very simple.

Mining

The Aztecs mined copper, gold, and silver and gemstones such as emeralds and amethysts, as well as the volcanic stone obsidian. Although there was plenty of iron in the soil, they did not know how to get it out.

Most metals are found as veins or particles in rocks, called ores. To get the ores out of the ground, Aztec miners dug out the rock and broke it up. They did this by pushing wooden wedges into cracks in the rock and pouring water over the wedges. As the water soaked into the wedges, the wood swelled and burst open the cracks. Sometimes the miners lit fires and heated the rock to make it crack.

Panning for Gold

To collect small particles and nuggets (lumps) of gold from river beds, the Aztecs used a method called panning. They filled a shallow wooden trough with water and sediment from the river, then swirled the mixture around. Any gold would sink to the bottom of the pan because it was much heavier than other sediments. The other materials would remain in the water and could be poured away.

Smelting

Metals must be refined, or purified, before they can be used. This is done by smelting, a process in which crushed ore is heated in a furnace to separate out the metals. The Aztecs smelted ores by packing them between layers of wood and charcoal and heating them to very high temperatures in a simple furnace. Fires need lots of oxygen to make them burn hot. There is oxygen in the air, so the Aztecs designed their furnaces to allow plenty of air to get in. Metalworkers blew through copper or reed blowpipes to make the fire burn very hot; this one is casting a copper axe head—the molten copper runs out of a hole in the furnace into a stone mold.

Arts and Crafts

Metalworking

The Aztecs used different techniques to make metal ornaments and jewelry. To make hollow or delicate metal shapes, they used a complicated process known as lost-wax casting. This method involved making an inner core out of charcoal and clay, which was covered with beeswax and smoothed and sculpted carefully to give the required shape. The shape was then covered with a layer of clay with a few holes in it and heated in an oven so that the wax melted and flowed out, leaving a hollow space or mold. The mold was then filled with molten silver or gold, and when it cooled, the mold was broken and the metal ornament taken out.

Gold and Silver Jewelry

The Aztecs made some metal objects by beating thin sheets of gold, silver, or copper. They made other ornaments and jewelry by pouring molten gold or silver into simple stone or pottery molds. In this picture Diego Rivera shows Aztecs as they might have worked in their workshops.

Making an Ornament Using Different Metals

Metalworkers used a special type of lost-wax casting to make ornaments with more than one metal. Working with different metals is difficult because, for instance, silver melts at a lower temperature than gold. First, the craftsman cast the gold part of the object. Then he made a wax model of the silver part and covered it with clay. He heated the clay so that the wax ran out, then poured in molten silver. Because silver melts at a lower temperature than gold, the gold stayed solid when the molten silver was added. This gold, silver, and turquoise pendant represents a shield with arrows.

An Embossed Golden Pendant

One method of jewelry making was to hammer the metal into sheets, cut it into shapes, and then decorate the shapes by embossing (pressing) designs into them from the back.

Make an Aztec Metal Pendant

You will need some plasticine, a rolling pin, a sheet of tinfoil, a pencil with a blunt point, scissors, and a sheet of thin cardboard.

1 Cut a circle from the cardboard to form a backing for the pendant and cut a circle out of the tinfoil at least 1 in. (2.5 cm) larger than the cardboard circle.

2 Roll out the plasticine to form a mat about 2 in. (5 cm) thick.

3 Lay the foil circle, shiny side down, on the plasticine. With the pencil, draw a design on the foil, gently pressing the foil into the plasticine. Don't press too hard, or the foil will tear. Pull the foil off the plasticine carefully. You will see your design pushed out on the shiny side of the foil.

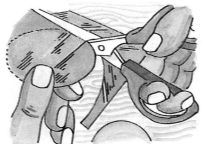

4 To strengthen your pendant, lay it on top of the cardboard circle and fold back the edges of the foil around the cardboard. You can hang it around your neck with a piece of string.

Decorations and Jewelry

The Aztecs loved bright colors. Their craftspeople, called lapidaries, worked with brilliant-colored stones such as jade, turquoise, and quartz. They carved and polished the stones and used them to make mosaics and jewelry and to decorate objects such as masks and weapons. The Aztecs also loved feathers; they used them to make headdresses as well as to decorate shields, banners, and luxury clothes.

Feather Decorations

The Aztecs used feather mosaics to decorate objects. Making a feather mosaic was a complicated process. First, the craftsperson used a stencil, probably cut out of a plant leaf, to transfer a design onto stiffened cloth. Next, the feathers were trimmed with a copper knife on a cutting board, dipped in glue made from resin obtained from plants, and stuck, one by one, onto the cloth, with a flat piece of bone used as a spatula. When the pattern was complete, the cloth was attached to a board.

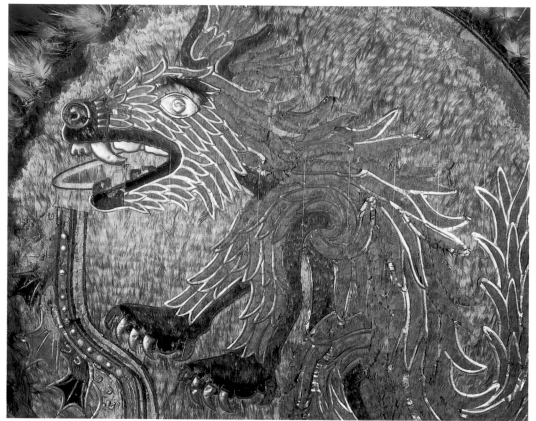

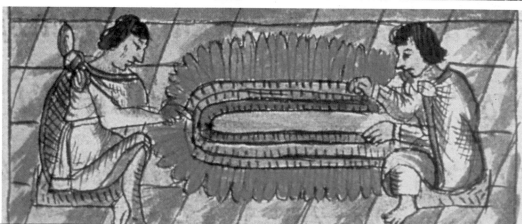

Carving Gemstones

Aztec lapidaries carved colored gemstones and shiny black obsidian. They used a copper tool to carve these hard stones and ground them with a mixture of sand and hard mineral fragments. They drilled tiny holes in the stones with little tubes made of copper, bone, or wood. They polished and smoothed the stones by rubbing them with fine sand and then with a piece of cane. This produced a smooth shiny surface that could be used as a mirror.

Turquoise and Shell Mosaics

Lapidaries used gemstone mosaics to decorate masks, knives, shields, and pottery. The mosaics were often made out of small pieces of turquoise combined with other colored stones and pieces of red or white shells. These were glued onto a backing, using a kind of cement, or sometimes beeswax. This Aztec mosaic mask was made by gluing pieces of turquoise and shell fragments onto a human skull with the back cut away.

Jewelry for Rich and Poor

All Aztecs, both men and women, loved to wear jewelry. They combined many of their craft technologies, including methods of metalworking, lapidary work, and leather work to make beads, necklaces, earrings, nose studs, and lip-plugs. Poor people wore jewelry made of cheap materials like this necklace made of shells and colored stones. Rich Aztecs wore jewelry made of gemstones or gold and silver.

Pottery

When the Spaniards arrived in Mexico they were astonished by the beautiful Aztec craft work they found. Aztec potters did not use a wheel, but with their very simple tools, they made fine, delicate, decorated pottery, as well as well-designed pots for people to use every day in their homes.

Pots for the Home

Aztec women used pottery for cooking and preparing food. Everyday pottery was very rough and plain, but it was carefully designed to do its job well. For example, the undersides of clay griddles were roughened so that they would distribute the heat more evenly. Cooking pots were often made by women who built up coils of clay by hand into the shape they wanted. Then they smoothed the surface of the pot, using sticks and leaves, before drying it in the sun.

Sometimes they decorated the dried pots, using a stick dipped in paint made of the soot of burned pine trees, before firing the pots in an open fire.

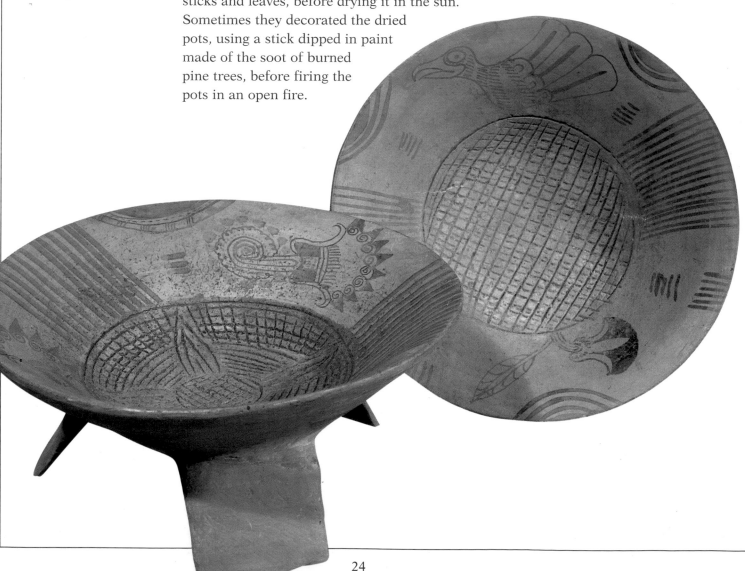

Special ornaments

Aztec potters also used their hands to make thinner and more delicate pottery for use in public buildings or in the houses of important people. These pieces were beautifully decorated with complicated designs, using colored paints made from crushed insects or the sap or resin from plants.

Make an Aztec Pot

Aztec potters built up their pots by coiling "ropes" of clay. After they had formed the pot, they smoothed it into shape with their hands.

You will need air-drying or modeling clay and acrylic paints.

1 Roll small lumps of clay on a tabletop, using your hands to make "ropes."

2 To make the bottom of the pot, start from the center, coiling the clay rope. As you form the bottom of your pot, you can join two pieces of clay rope by pressing their ends together.

3 When you have made the bottom of the pot the size you want, start building up the sides by laying the rope coils on top of each other and pressing them together.

4 Smooth your finished pot with your hands. Leave it to dry and harden in a warm room or outside in the sun. When the pot is completely dry, you can decorate it with paint.

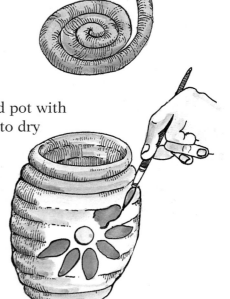

Health

Herbal Medicine

Aztec doctors, or healers, used a mixture of magic, religion, and medicines to cure their patients. Their medicines came mainly from plants, and many of these plant remedies are still used today.

Healers used about 1,300 different plants to produce herbal medicines. For example, they used a type of southernwood (*Artemesia*) for cooling fevers and curing coughs and a type of passionflower (*Passiflora*) as a remedy for snake bite. They also developed herbal medicines to stop bleeding, to calm people with fits, heal skin problems, and cure many other illnesses.

Botanical Gardens

The Aztecs set up botanical gardens, similar to ones grown today. These provided useful plants for making medicines. Healers treated their patients by using a mixture of herbal medicines and sound common sense. For example, to cure a hoarse voice, one doctor recommended: "Many times the throat is massaged with liquid rubber. And bee honey is to be drunk, and many times, by way of the nose, bee honey or thickened maguey syrup will drop into the throat." Many people today use a similar medicine to soothe sore throats—syrups or lozenges made of honey and lemon.

Herbal Remedies

Scientists have studied many of the herbal remedies used by the Aztecs and have shown that they worked. That is because the plants used by Aztec healers contain chemical substances that can fight disease.

Today, many people still prefer to use herbal remedies to cure their illnesses. Chemical drug companies, too, are interested in herbal medicines because many plants contain substances that turn out to be useful drugs. Aspirin, which was originally discovered in the bark of a certain type of willow tree, is just one example.

Aztec Herbals

To explain the different herbs and methods they used to cure people, healers wrote "medical dictionaries," called herbals. These described the various plants and their uses. Herbals contained information about how to make medicines from different plants, such as *Passiflora* (left) and suggested what diseases the medicines could cure. They included very clear pictures of useful plants so that people could recognize them.

Make Your Own Herbal

Draw a picture of a common plant, such as a marigold, whose botanical name is *Calendula officinalis*. Label any features you think will help people to recognize it. Then use this information to make up some pages for your herbal. The secret of a good herbal is to arrange the page so that the information is easy to find.

An infusion of marigolds is often good for treating small cuts or burns. First dry the marigold flowers, then chop them up. Pour boiling water over them to make a strong infusion (like tea). When the infusion is cool, it can be used as a lotion.

You can make up herbal pages for other plants that are used as medicines.

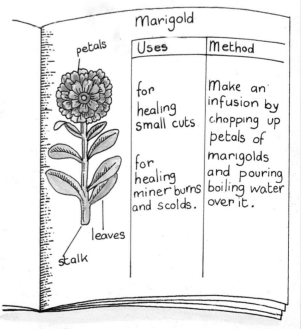

Marigold

petals

Uses	Method
for healing small cuts	Make an infusion by chopping up petals of marigolds and pouring boiling water over it.
for healing miner burns and scolds.	

leaves

stalk

Treating the Sick

The Aztecs did not suffer too much from common illnesses, such as infections and stomach upsets, until Cortés and his troops arrived. The Spaniards brought with them many new diseases such as measles, typhoid, smallpox, and yellow fever. The Aztecs had no resistance to these, and even a fairly mild attack could kill. Although their herbal medicines helped in some cases, thousands of Aztecs died from these diseases, brought to their country from Europe.

Steam Baths

The Aztecs believed that steam was a useful treatment for minor problems such as stiff muscles, blotchy complexions, and coughs and chills. They also thought that hot, steamy rooms helped pregnant women to deliver their babies more easily. An Aztec steam bath was a room built out of stone. A furnace was lit against one of the outside walls. When the walls of the stone room were hot, they were splashed with water to produce steam.

Cutting and Bleeding

Although Aztec healers did not carry out surgical operations, they used sharp obsidian blades to cut open boils and abcesses. If this did not relieve the pain, they made a cut near the swelling to let the patient bleed. Bleeding was also used to help cure headaches and inflamed joints. To stop bleeding, they sewed up wounds using cactus spines as needles and hair as thread.

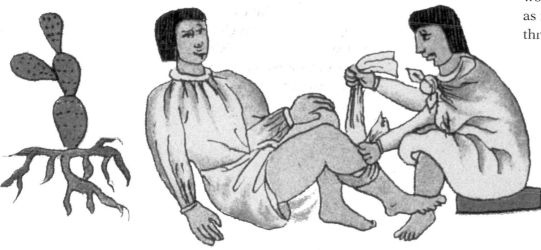

Setting Bones

Healers also knew how to treat people with broken bones. They pushed the patient's bones back into place with their hands and tied on splints to keep the limb from moving while the bones grew back together.

Travel

Roads and Canals

The Aztecs built roads in many of their cities to make it easier for people to get around. Speaking of Tenochtitlán, a Spanish soldier described how some main streets were "half of hard earth like a pavement and the other half is water." Other main "streets," he said, were "entirely of water, and all travel is by backs and canoes."

Aztec merchants traveled all over Central America, bringing back goods for the city markets. They used a network of long-distance routes that linked the main towns. Relays of runners were used to carry letters, and they also brought fresh foods such as fish from the coasts to Tenochtitlán. By passing the goods from runner to runner and traveling day and night, the runners could cover 155 mi. (250 km) in twenty-four hours. When Cortés and his soldiers landed in Mexico, relays of runners kept the Aztec Emperor Montezuma in touch with the Spaniards' every move.

Long-Distance Road Networks

One important long-distance route was the road that ran between Tenochtitlán and Xicalango and other trading cities on the coast of the Gulf of Mexico. Another route linked Tenochtitlán with the Pacific coast, ending just south of Acapulco.

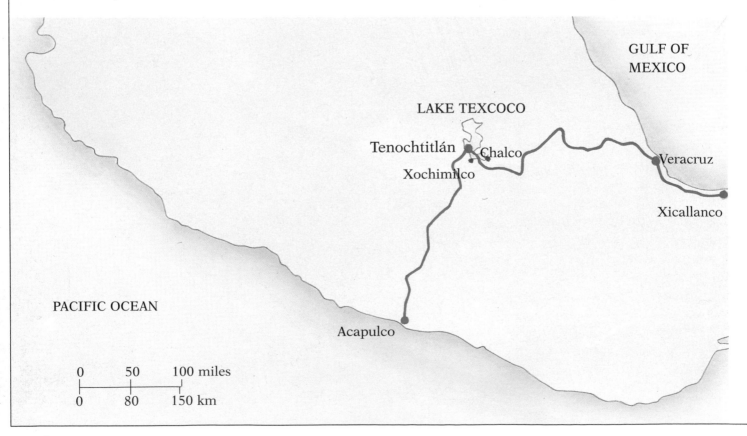

GULF OF MEXICO

LAKE TEXCOCO

Tenochtitlán · Chalco

Xochimilco

Veracruz

Xicallanco

PACIFIC OCEAN

Acapulco

| 0 | 50 | 100 miles |
| 0 | 80 | 150 km |

Maintaining the Roads

The long-distance roads were simply dirt tracks through the jungle. Aztec road-builders cut steps into the steeper parts to make them easier to travel along and to prevent the tracks from being washed away during heavy rain. Aztecs living near the roads kept them clear, cutting down plants and removing fallen trees throughout the year. After the rainy season they repaired the road surface and filled in potholes. They built rest houses, shelters, and even public lavatories along the way, and these were kept in good repair because each roadside village was responsible for taking care of 20 mi. (32 km) of roadway.

Canals and Waterways

Traveling by boat was a good way to move people and goods. Long-distance canals connected towns in the Valley of Mexico. A canal connected Tenochtitlán with towns on neighboring lakes and continued on to the cities of Xochimilco and Chalaco. The canals were 15 to 40 ft. (4.5 to 12 m) wide. They were sometimes cut through reed beds and had to be cleared often to keep them open.

Carrying Goods and People

Because the Aztecs had no pack animals or carts, all their goods had to be carried, either on their backs or in boats that they propelled along their canals. On land, they carried their loads in special backpacks, and on the canals they used simple dugout canoes with upturned ends.

Building Canoes

Aztec canoes were carved from tree trunks. Most canoes had plain, upturned ends, but the prow of a noble's canoe was carved in the shape of an eagle. Boatbuilders used copper or stone-headed tools to make all-purpose canoes about 13 ft. (4 m) long. These carried about five people or a small load of goods. Some canoes were much larger— more than 50 ft. (15 m) long—and could carry up to 60 passengers or 3 tons of corn. The boatman propelled the boat along, standing near the stern and using a pole or paddle.

Porters

Merchants hired teams of porters to transport their goods. The porters normally carried loads of as much as 60 lbs. (27 kg) over distances of about 15 mi. (24 km) each day. These heavy weights were carried in backpacks. The load was tied to a carrying frame made of two strong upright poles placed about a body's width apart. The frame was held together by horizontal crosspieces that were tied on with rope, made of braided fibers.

For support, instead of shoulder straps, an Aztec backpack had a rope that went around the porter's forehead.

What Is the Easiest Way to Carry a Load?

The Aztecs took the weight of their backpacks using a band around their foreheads, instead of using shoulder straps. Try this experiment and see whether a forehead band makes a load easier to carry.

You will need a backpack with a metal frame, some books or other items weighing about 4 to 7 lbs. (2 to 3 kg), and a strip of strong cloth about 5 ft. (1.5 m) long, to use as a forehead strap.

1 Put the books in the backpack and put the backpack on your back in the normal way, using the shoulder straps. Walk around the room several times. Consider how heavy the weights feel. Now try the Aztec system (step 2).

2 Tie the cloth strip around one side of the backpack frame near the top. Ask someone to hold the backpack against your back and help you to pass the strip around your forehead and tie it securely to the other side of the backpack frame. Don't put your arms through the shoulder straps. Instead, try carrying the load with the weight balanced by the forehead strap. See if the weights are easier to carry this way.

Warfare

Weapons

Aztec Throwing Spears

Warriors used long spears, which they hurled at enemy soldiers. These powerful spears were hardened by fire at one end and sharpened to a fierce point, or had heads of deadly chipped obsidian.

The Aztecs developed a powerful civilization, but their gods demanded human sacrifices. One way to satisfy the gods was to provide a supply of prisoners of war as sacrificial victims. Because of their need to make war on neighboring tribes, the Aztecs developed many different types of weapons, made of stone, bone, and wood. All Aztec weapons were very simple, but when used by skillful warriors, they were very effective. In addition to their weapons of war, the Aztecs used special weapons for hunting. They shot animals with clay pellets fired through blowguns made of hollow copper tubes or long reeds.

The *Atlatl*

Warriors threw their spears by using a spear-thrower, or a*tlatl*. The *atlatl* helped hurl the spear over a long distance. It was made of a flat piece of wood up to 2 ft. (60 cm) long. The spear was placed in a groove at one end, and the warrior held the *atlatl* at the other end. This arrangement extended his arm and allowed him to hurl the spear with greater force over a longer distance than simply throwing it by hand.

Slings, Bows, and Arrows

The Aztecs also used slings to hurl stones at their enemies. They collected the stones before battle and carefully ground and rounded them so that they could be aimed very accurately. The slings were made of maguey fibers or braided cotton. Aztec bows were of wood, about 5 ft. (1.5 m) long, with strings made of animal sinews or strips of deerskin. Arrows were made of reeds that had been straightened and smoothed by heating over a fire. The ends of the arrows were bound with maguey fiber to keep them from splitting. Sharp arrow heads made of obsidian were glued to one end, using resin. Feathers were arranged on the other end of the arrow so that it would fly in a straight line.

Hand-to-Hand Fighting

Aztec warriors used spears or swords to thrust and to slash and clubs to strike out at their enemies. They wore padded armor, helmets, and shields to protect themselves. Their armor was thick but much more comfortable and effective than the steel armor worn by the Spaniards. Their shields often had feather fringes at the bottom, which, although appearing fragile, gave good protection to the legs.

Warriors fought their enemies with short wooden swords and spears so sharp they could use them to shave their heads and beards. The Spaniards were amazed to find that Aztec swords were stronger and more deadly than their own metal swords. Their wooden clubs had heads surrounded by stone blades. Other clubs had a round ball made of stone attached to the end.

An Aztec Warrior Ready to Go into Battle

Helmet made of wood and bone

Shield, of split bamboo and maguey fiber strengthened with thick bamboo sticks, could be rolled up when not used, and unrolled quickly when needed. Other simple shields were of animal skin stretched over a wooden frame.

Wooden sword about 3 ft. (1 m) long and 4 in. (10 cm) wide, with obsidian or flint blades glued along the edge

Armor made from layers of quilted cotton stitched together with a leather border. The 2-in. (5-cm) thick padding could not be pierced by arrows or swords.

An Aztec Noble's Shield

This Aztec shield is made of tiny pieces of colored stone arranged in a mosaic. It was glued onto a leather backing with resin.

Battle Communications

When fighting began, trumpets and drumbeats could not be heard in the din, so Aztec commanders carried a standard or flag to show their warriors which way the troops were moving.

Make an Eagle Helmet

Sometimes an Aztec helmet resembled a bird or animal's head, and the warrior looked out through its open beak or jaws. Eagle knights wore eagle helmets.

You need two pieces of cardboard, 12 x 16 in. (40 cm x 30 cm); a long strip of cardboard about 1 in. (3 cm) wide, to secure your helmet over the top and back of your head and under your chin; pencil, scissors, and tape.

1 Draw the profile of an eagle on a piece of cardboard. Make it big enough to hide your head.

2 Cut out the drawing and lay it on the second piece of cardboard. Cut around this to make the second side of the head. Paint in the eagle's profile on both pieces of cardboard.

3 Ask a friend to help you tape the cardboard strips to the inside of your helmet so that it fits tightly on your head.

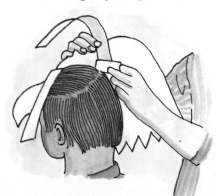

4 Put the helmet on your head and get your friend to tape both sides of the beak together in front of your chin.

Astronomy and Astrology

The Aztec View of the Universe

The Earth surrounded by water with Tenochtitlán surrounded by Texcoco Lake, the thirteen layers of heavens, and the nine layers of the underworld

Aztec Beliefs

Like many people today, the Aztecs observed the stars and planets in the night sky and wondered about their own place in the universe. Aztec ideas of the universe were very different from ours and were closely linked with their religion. They believed that the earth was surrounded by a large ring of water and above the earth were thirteen layers of the heavens. The lower layers of the heavens included the sky, stars, and planets, and the upper layers were the homes of the gods. Below the earth, they believed, were nine layers of the underworld. After death, people who had lived good lives or had died in a good cause went to the heavens. However, most people, they believed, went to the underworld, where they had to struggle hard to reach their final resting place in the ninth layer.

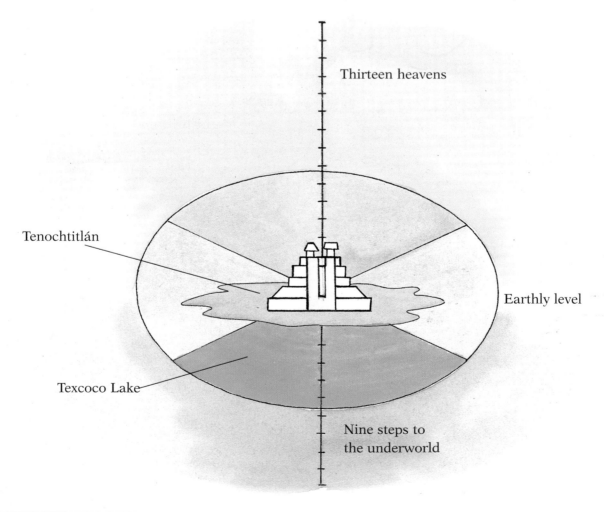

Thirteen heavens

Tenochtitlán

Earthly level

Texcoco Lake

Nine steps to the underworld

Astronomer Priests

Aztec priests had no telescopes to help them study the sky. Instead, they used a pair of crossed sticks. By looking through the sticks, the priests could be sure they were always looking at the sky from the same point. Using this fixed viewpoint made it easier to figure out how the stars and planets moved around each other. To make sure they had a clear view of the horizon, they set up the sticks high off the ground in their pyramid temples. By observing the night sky, Aztec priests learned how to predict eclipses. They also studied the patterns of the stars. They recognized many of the constellations and gave them names. They figured out the length of the year on the planet Venus by observing how the planet moved across the sky and counting the days until it returned to its original position.

Predicting the Future

One reason the Aztecs were so interested in the heavens was because they believed in astrology, the idea that movements of the stars and planets could be used to help predict the future. To help them in this work, they made up a Book of Days, the *Tonalamatl*. This page from the *Tonalamatl* records Aztec religious ceremonies. In the center is the god of fire. The dots indicate the days in the religious year. The Aztecs used dots for numbers less than twenty. They used different symbols for higher numbers.

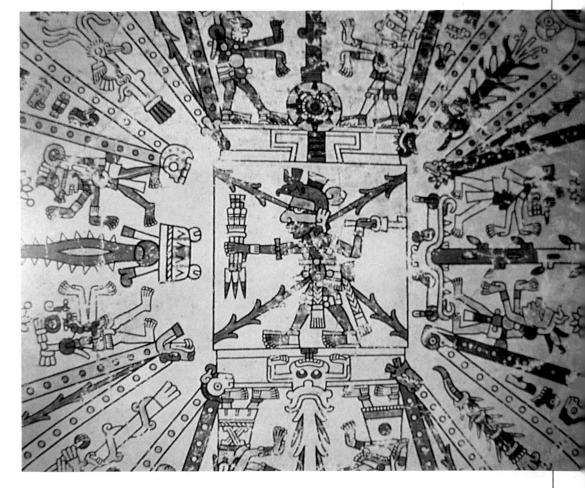

Measuring Time

The Solar and Sacred Calendars

Measuring time was very important to the Aztecs. The observations made by their priests helped them develop two different types of calendars. The solar (sun) calendar was worked out by studying the movement of the earth around the sun. It was used for planning the planting and harvesting of crops. The sacred, or holy, calendar was used for planning religious festivals.

The Bundle of Years

The Aztec solar calendar, like our own calendar, followed the movement of the earth around the sun. The Aztec year lasted just a few hours more than 365 days and was divided into 18 months of 20 days. Every year there were five days left over that belonged to no month. The Aztecs believed that these were unlucky days. A new age, or "bundle of years," began every 52 years. Priests kept count of the years by saving a special reed for each year. This carving represents a bundle of 52 sticks, which were burned at the fire festival at the end of a 52-year period.

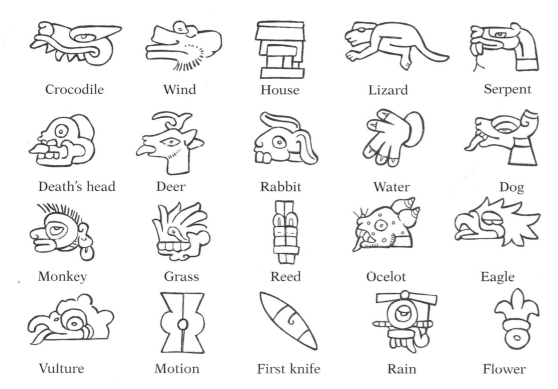

Crocodile Wind House Lizard Serpent

Death's head Deer Rabbit Water Dog

Monkey Grass Reed Ocelot Eagle

Vulture Motion First knife Rain Flower

The 20 Days of the Sacred Calendar

The Aztec religious year had 260 days in it and was divided into four months of 65 days each. The months were divided into five weeks of 13 days each. In the sacred calendar, each day in the year was given a name and a number and had a different meaning. There were 20 day-signs (shown here), each described by a glyph, or picture symbol (see also page 43).

The Calendar Stone

The Aztecs believed that they were living in the fifth and last world. In order to figure out the date when the world would end, they carved a huge, disk-shaped calendar stone. Instead of mapping out a single year, the calendar stone mapped out the time between the beginning and the ending of the world.

Reading and Writing

Codices

The Aztecs did not have an alphabet, but they did read and write. Instead of letters they used pictures. They produced thousands of "books," called codices, but only a few have survived. The codices are difficult to read, but they give us a great deal of information about how the Aztecs lived.

Picture Writing

Instead of using letters to form words, the Aztecs drew pictures, called glyphs. Using pointed sticks and ink made out of soot, they drew the outlines of their pictures in black and filled them in with pigments (colors) made with plants. When they wrote about something important, they drew a bigger picture. Sometimes the picture showed an object like a temple or palace. Or it might express an idea. For example, a line of footprints might mean travel. Pictures were also used to represent sounds. These sounds were combined to make a word. All three systems were often combined on one page, so reading an Aztec book was a bit like solving a puzzle.

Scribes

Skilled readers and writers, called scribes, wrote the codices. There were special scribes for different subjects. For example, one scribe would write about important events that took place each year; another would write about religious ceremonies. This painting by Diego Rivera shows the scribes writing their codices and illustrates the importance of the priests (in the foreground).

Paper and Papermaking

The scribes used almost 500,000 sheets of paper every year, so papermaking was an important industry. The Aztecs made paper by soaking the bark of fig trees in water with limestone dissolved in it to loosen the fibers. Then, they beat the fibers with a bark-beater—a large stone held with a willow handle. Finally, they glued the fibers together with resin and used the bark-beater again to flatten them into a thin sheet of paper that they smoothed and dried. The paper was very rough, so the scribes coated it with a chalk paste to make it easier to write on.

bark beater

bark fibers

Producing Codices

The scribes wrote their codices on long strips of paper about 6 in. (15 cm) wide and up to 40 ft. (12 m) long. They wrote on both sides of the strip and used red or black lines to divide the book into pages. When the book was written, it was folded in a zigzag, like a map. The ends of the strip were glued to thin pieces of wood, which were sometimes decorated with paintings or gemstones. When readers opened the book, they could see two pages at once. They read the pages from top to bottom and from left to right, as we do.

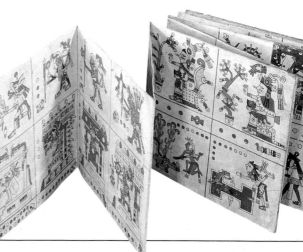

43

Technology Through Time

before A.D. 1100	The Aztecs, a small nomadic tribe, roam thoughout Middle America.
ca. 1100 to 1200	Toltecs building temples and other ceremonial architecture from stone. Development of the Sacred Calendar.
1150	Destruction of the Toltec city of Tula, in Central Mexico.
ca. 1168	The Aztecs and other tribes move into the area but have no land of their own. The Aztecs begin searching for a place to settle.
1345	The Aztecs settle on an island in the middle of Lake Texcoco in the Valley of Mexico. They are ruled by another city-state, Azcapotzalco.
ca. 1348	The Aztecs begin building Tenochtitlán, sinking piles into lake marshes to form foundations for the city. They begin building *chinampas*. Cultivation of corn and other crops for food and maguey cactus and cotton for clothes.
1428	The Aztecs defeat the rulers of Azcapotzalco.
1431	Tenochtitlán becomes an independent state in alliance with neighboring cities of Texcoco and Tlacopán.
ca. 1450s	Mining of minerals and gemstones. Manufacture of jewelry, mosaics, and plain pottery. Development of trade. Copper begins to be used for tools.
ca. 1455	Lost-wax method of casting metals first used.
1440	Montezuma I becomes emperor.

ca. 1442	Aqueducts built to bring drinking water to Tenochtitlán.
	Dike built to east of Tenochtitlán to reduce floods.
ca. 1450s	Many temples and public buildings built in Tenochtitlán and Texcoco.
1468	Under rule of Montezuma I, the Aztec empire extends from the Atlantic to the Pacific. Four hundred ninety-eight cities pay tribute (taxes).
	Routes built across the empire.
1500s	Fine decorated pottery first crafted.
1502	Montezuma II becomes emperor.
1519	Spanish explorer Hernando Cortés lands on the east coast of Mexico with an army.
1521	Tenochtitlán is captured by Cortés and his soldiers, bringing about the downfall and ending of the Aztec empire.

Glossary

Abscesses Swellings caused by an infection.

Alliance Official agreement between nations or tribes.

Alum A mineral that contains the chemicals potassium and aluminum.

Amethyst A purple gemstone.

Aqueducts Raised channels for carrying water.

Archaeologists Scientists who dig up and study the remains of ancient cities and settlements.

Astrology The nonscientific study of the movements and positions of the planets in the hope of foretelling the future.

Astronomy The scientific study of stars, planets, and other heavenly bodies. An astronomer is someone who studies astronomy.

Canals Channels filled with water for boats to travel on.

Causeways Raised roads across marshy ground or water.

Constellations Groups of stars.

Eclipse The cutting off of light from the sun when the moon comes between the sun and the earth—or the similar eclipse of the moon when the shadow of the earth falls on it.

Fertile Able to produce plentiful plants and seeds.

Furnace A large oven that can be heated to high temperatures.

Gemstones Semiprecious minerals.

Glyphs The pictures the Aztecs used for their writing.

Grid A regular, square, or rectangular pattern.

Griddle A flat disk of clay or metal used for cooking.

Herbal remedies Medicines produced from chemicals in plants.

Herbals Books that describe plants and their healing properties.

Irrigate To water land by means of canals, ditches, etc.

Kernels The seeds of wheat or corn, inside a hard husk.

Mosaics Pictures or patterns made by sticking small pieces of colored stone onto a backing.

Maguey Cactus A type of cactus growing in Mexico. Its leaves had many uses for the Aztecs.

Predict To foretell the future.

Resin A kind of sap from plants and trees.

Sacrifices Offerings to gods. The Aztecs believed their gods demanded the sacrifice of human beings.

Sediment Small particles of sand, mud, and rock.

Solar calendar A calendar based on observations of the time it takes for the earth to travel around the sun. Our own calendar is made up in this way, and like the Aztec calendar, our year is slightly longer than 365 days.

Spatula A blunt flat blade used for spreading.

Spindle A thin rod on which thread is twisted and wound in spinning.

Splints Rods or sticks used to give broken limbs support while they heal.

Stencil A cut-out pattern used to transfer a design.

Thatch A roofing material made of straw or leaves, held in place with rope made out of the same material.

Varnish A thin coating painted onto a surface to make it smooth and shiny.

Volcanic rocks Rocks formed in volcanoes. They are usually very hard.

Warp The threads that run through the length of cloth.

Wattle and daub Building materials made by weaving together sticks and twigs and covering them with mud.

Weft The threads that run across the width of the cloth.

Yarn Thick threads made out of twisted fibers.

Books to Read

Arnold, Caroline. *Mexico's Ancient City of Teotihuacan*. New York: Clarion Books, 1994.

Berdan, Frances F. *The Aztecs* (Indians of North America.) New York: Chelsea House, 1989.

Bierhorst, John (ed.) *The Hungry Woman: Myths and Legends of the Aztecs*. New York: Morrow Junior Books, 1993.

Dawson, Imogen. *Food and Feasts with the Aztecs* (Food & Feasts.) Parsippany, NJ: Silver Burdett Press, 1995.

Dineen, Jacqueline. *The Aztecs* (Worlds of the Past.) Parsippany, NJ: Silver Burdett Press, 1992.

Hicks, Peter. *The Aztecs* (Look Into the Past.) Austin, TX: Thomson Learning, 1993.

Patent, Dorothy H. *The Quetzal: Sacred Bird of the Forest*. New York: Morrow Junior Books, 1996.

Shepherd, Donna A. *The Aztecs*. (First Book.) Danbury, CT: Franklin Watts, 1992.

Picture acknowledgments

The pictures in this book were supplied by AKG London 9, 37(lower); Ancient Art and Architecture Collection 19(top), 39(lower); Bridgeman Art Library 7, 22(lower), 32, 34; ET Archive 8, 16, 28, 29; Mexicolore title page, 20, 21(top), 17(top), 31(lower), 43(top); Oxford Scientific Films 26; Edward Parker 4, 10; South American PIctures 11(both), 27, 31(top); Wayland Picture Library 15, 19(lower), 23(center), 37(top), 39(top), 44, 45; Werner Forman Archive cover, 6, 15, 21(lower), 22(top), 23(top and lower), 24, 25, 40, 41(lower), 42, 43(lower). Cover artwork by Christa Hook; map artwork by John Yates.

Index

Page numbers in **bold** indicate that there is information about the subject in a photograph or diagram.